Table Contents

Introduction

Architecture is more than just being the science of home design. It is not just about the length of lines, the way houses should be built, the number of floors or rooms to make, and the strategic location of the house you are going to design. Architecture is an art. To become a successful architect means to make use of the knowledge of how the history of human civilization has shaped the way we live, and in effect, the shape of the homes in which we live.

This book was specifically made with the fledgling architect in mind, thoroughly discussing everything that an architect should know, from the history of architectural development to the different types of lines and tools needed in order to create architectural masterpieces. It arms architects-to-be and architect wannabes with the basic skills and knowledge required of every single architect in the world.

Thanks for buying this book. I hope you like it!

Chapter 1: Architecture As An Art

Everywhere we look, especially in cities, we see houses, office buildings, shopping malls, parks, schools, hotels, and other infrastructures. Subliminally we judge how these buildings look, how they strike us with their style and grandeur, and how they evoke certain feelings and emotions.

Buildings hold meaning for us, based not only on what we did in them or what happened within their premises, but also on their looks. In admiring the glorious works of architecture, we think of the people behind the design of the magnificent towers of the modern urban cities, and the beautiful homes in rural or suburban areas, the great designers who came up with these structures, who used their creative imaginations to build these fantastic wonders of mankind.

These people, the architects, are responsible for the creative use of the spaces in which we live, work, and learn. Although it may seem like a glamorous job – using the magic of the mind to create a perfect piece of architecture that can be appreciated by generations to come – it actually takes a lot of hard work.

Architecture is not only an art, but it is also a science. Architecture involves a lot of the same math as trigonometry, requiring the same amount of creative juice as the fine arts, and needing as much wit and intelligence as the great works of literature. Not only that, architecture adheres to a lot of sciences, both real and pseudo. Great architects have followed the ways of religious institutions, have made sure that certain beliefs are respected, and have even adhered to pseudo sciences such as Feng Shui, such as when asking questions like to which direction should the house be pointed at, how many floors should it have (Should we skip the 13th floor?) or in which location is construction best done.

If you are a beginner, the first thing that you must realize is that architecture is not easy, and truly mastering does not happen overnight. Architecture requires full passion, full commitment, and full attention at all times. Great architects have preserved their designed buildings like great monuments or paintings from classical eras. If you dream of being in the line of the greats, you must pay close attention to the very basics.

Here, therefore, is where this book comes in. As you read this book on architecture, you will realize the vastness of the field which you have decided to pursue. This world will both excite you with the possibilities that it will hold, and it will make you worry about the future and what you, as a future architect, will contribute for the benefit of the art of architecture.

You will be walked through the basics of architecture, such as the concepts which you must always bear in mind, to the common practices that most architects adhere to when they are designing structures, regardless if these are for commercial or private use. Once you have completed this book, you will have everything you need to elevate yourself to become a great architect in the future.

Welcome to the world of architecture!

Chapter 2: History Of Architecture

Architecture, or the art of structure design, has been around for an inordinate amount of time, and has developed along with other aspects of human society, including religion, art, and language. The design of homes and monuments that were built by ancient civilizations were definitely affected by a lot of factors like location and culture. Abodes for both the rich and the poor reflected the beliefs of the people during their respective eras, and signified the color and uniqueness of their cultures. The most ancient forms of architecture formed the basis for later architectural styles, and up to this day, traces of ancient architecture can still be seen in the design of the homes where we now live.

Before we discuss the basics of becoming an architect, it is important to first acquire a clear understanding of the evolution of architecture, from the stone structures of ancient Egypt to the modern designs of today's famous architects.

Both the arts and architecture have gone hand in hand in change and development throughout the course of history. These two significant facets of human society share a strong bond for three simple reasons.

1. Heads of state in the ancient times who commissioned the construction of public structures had aesthetics or looks, especially for religious buildings, and functionality in mind. Buildings were created to both inspire those who will see them, and also to serve their intended purposes. As a result of this, the creation of buildings also involved the help of decorative labourers and craftsmen.

2. A lot of the buildings created in the earlier period of our history until the post-Renaissance period also served as a sort of canvas where murals were painted, acting like a showcase for some of the most beautiful works of fine art. Everything from paintings to sculptures and stained glass were included in the construction of the buildings.

3. The construction of public buildings generally developed alongside the development of visual arts, specifically during certain art movements such as the Renaissance, Rococo, Baroque, and Neoclassical periods, which influenced how buildings were designed for their aesthetic purposes.

Beginning with ancient architecture, building design had only two functions: 1) to show the wealth and power of the ruling class where that building was constructed; and 2) to please the deities which were worshipped by the civilization who made the buildings.

- One of the very first ancient civilizations to rise was the Egyptian civilization. This civilization grew to become the first of many great civilizations to rise from the Mediterranean, around 3100 to 2040 BCE. The Egyptians were famous for not only their unique pieces of architecture, but also for their introduction and use of written language, an absolute monarchy, and a well established religion.

Today, they are remembered for their most significant contribution to the architectural and artistic world—the Pyramids of Giza. The architectural style of the Egyptians focused on being big. Their works were massive in size and definitely imposed the feeling of power and wealth. However, although the architectural wonders of the Egyptians were known for being large, they were not necessarily complicated, as they are only made of piled stone bricks and posts instead of arches. Eventually other civilizations drew inspiration from their works, most notably the Greeks.

- Sumerian Architecture developed in one of the most important cradles of human civilization, Mesopotamia. With the Egyptians having their own thing going on when it comes to architecture, especially with the creation of their pyramids, the Sumerians also became busy creating their own unique architectural wonders.

The Sumerians are remembered today as the creators of pyramids with steps called the Ziggurat. If the Egyptian pyramids were created in order to serve as the home of their dead rulers, the Ziggurat of the Sumerians were used to bring the people of the Sumerian civilization, as well as their rulers, closer to their gods. Therefore, this piece of architecture had more of a religious function, sort of like how churches are used today. The Sumerian Ziggurats were created with the use of bricks made from fire-dried clay, which were then finished by using colored glazes.

- In southern Europe, the ancient Greeks were also known as one of the finest ancient civilizations to have ever lived. The Greeks were not only responsible for the mythology that we know today, as well as the concept of democracy, but they are also responsible for one of the most complex forms of ancient architecture in the world.

Greek Architecture is wide and extremely complicated. It can basically be divided into three fundamental eras: Archaic (600-500 BCE), Classical (500-323 BCE) and the Hellenistic (323-27 BCE) Eras. In 600 BCE, upon taking inspiration from the architectural wonders of the Egyptians, the Greeks decided to gradually replace their wooden buildings with stone structures. This process was known as "petrification," and it involved the use of marble and limestone for the creation of walls and columns, and terracotta for ornaments and roof tiles. As for decorations, they were made using metals such as bronze. The buildings made by the Greeks included temples, theatres, stadiums, and government buildings.

During the time of the ancient Greeks, fame was not something that their artists got to enjoy, unlike the case of the artists we have today. They were not seen as artists during their time, but rather as tradesmen. Therefore, there are almost no known names of architects who built the great infrastructures of ancient Greece before the 5th century BCE.

Post and lintel techniques in building infrastructures were the main methods used by the ancient Greeks. Although they were able to construct magnificent buildings with what they knew, they still did not know enough about how to make larger spaces without using more materials for support. The Romans who will come after them will eventually develop the arch, which will help in eliminating the need for more columns. For the Greeks, the larger the structure to be built, the more columns needed to be used. Basic formats of construction included the use of large amounts of limestone, as well as tuff, a stone with lighter weight. Marble, unlike limestone, was difficult to find in large amounts, and therefore was more valuable. Due to its impracticality, the Greeks reserved marble for sculptures, except for very important buildings such as the Acropolis's Parthenon.

The design of ancient Greek architecture consists of a rectangular building design, which is then covered by columns on all sides such as in the Parthenon. In rare cases, there would only be columns on the front and back of the building, such as in the Temple of Athena Nike. Roofs had terracotta tiles, and they were always flat. Changes happened during the late 4th and 5th centuries BCE, when the architects at the time decided to create circular buildings called tholos. These circular buildings were beautifully adorned with black marble, and there were large, magnificent sculptures displayed along the building's sides.

Greek architecture theories were heavily drawn from the system of the Classical orders, which is what basically sets the rules for the construction of a building's basic parts. There are three orders:

- Doric – This was a common architectural style in mainland Greece which was later adapted by Greek colonies in modern day Italy. It is characterized as being very simple, sturdy, austere, and formal. This was the most popular form of architecture during the Classical Age, with the Temple of Hephasetus being a prime example.

- Ionic – This architectural style was dominant in structures built in Turkey's west coast, as well as in other Aegean islands. Unlike the rigid Doric style, the Ionic was more fluid and open for decorations. This became popular with the coming of the Hellenistic Era.

- ○ Corinthian – This was the architectural style to appear last in Greek architecture, and evolved as an even more ornate form of the Ionic style. Corinthian structures were highly decorative.

- The Romans were remarkably more different from the Greeks which preceded them. The Romans, unlike the intellectual and creative Greeks, were more concerned with matters of the military, construction, and engineering. The artistic side of the Romans heavily drew inspiration from the Etruscans and their inventions of very efficient machines for hydraulics, and the Greeks, who they consider as their superiors in all aspects of the arts. Although even the Romans conceded that the Greeks were orders of magnitude better than them when it comes to the arts, they were the ones responsible for bringing awareness of the greatness of Greek architecture to the world, and in effect, to history. Without the intervention of the Romans, Greek architecture would have been eternally lost.

The main purpose of Roman architecture was to serve the Roman state's needs. The Roman Empire was a nation that grew at a really fast pace, and people tended to live close to each other, forming large cities. This created a problem for engineers and architects on how they are going to solve not only housing, but also security and drainage problems. With thousands of people calling one city their home, the demand for clean and drinkable water increased. Along with the dream of the Romans to make themselves the greatest civilization on earth and of proving that fact to the world, architects dreamed big and created megastructures (at the time) to satisfy the needs of the people in the cities.

Architectural achievements by the Romans included, among other things, more than eleven aqueducts in Rome alone, such as Aqua Novus and Aqua Claudia, roads, bridges, public areas such as baths (including the Baths of Diocletian and Caracalla), ampitheaters (the most important example of which is the Colosseum of Rome, built from 72-80 CE), sports facilities, and even centralized systems for heating. In addition to these feats, theatres and religious temples were also created.

With the expansion of the Roman Empire, architects saw more chances to design and create towns from nothing, simply basing their designs on a grid plan which included two main streets: an east-west axis (decumanus) and north-south axis (cardo). The very center of the town would be located at the meeting point of the two roads.

Roman architecture is remembered for their introduction of the arch. In addition to new and improved designs from existing patterns from the Greeks, the Romans were also responsible for the creation of new building materials such as concrete. Concrete, or opus cementicium to the Romans, was originally made of stones, sand, water, and mortar, and was a very strong replacement for stone when the latter was not available in large amounts for construction purposes.

Arches were crucial in improving the capabilities and efficiency of the aqueducts and bridges of the cities. The invention of the arch also made it possible to create larger interior spaces, which was virtually impossible during the time of the Greeks.

Just like the Egyptians and the Greeks, the Romans also made sure that their iconic infrastructures were also adorned with a variety of beautiful artworks such as sculptures (specifically statues, reliefs, and busts of the reigning Emperor), mosaics, and murals.

- The Romans were in power for a very long time and managed to spread their influence in mainland Europe. However, due to power struggles and difficulties maintaining a strong leadership within the country, the Roman Empire eventually collapsed. With the fall of one of the greatest nations in the world, turmoil followed suit. During this time until the 11th century, the next major architectural movement was born.

The Romanesque style was dominantly seen as the emerging style of designing Catholic churches during the period after the Romans until before the 1200s. The Romanesque design somewhat drew from both Greek and Roman traditions. However, since the leading designers of Romanesque churches did not have the same intellect as the Greeks nor the same abilities in engineering as the Romans, they were left to simply draw inspiration from their works.

This style used very thick walls, piers, round shaped arches, narrow slit windows, columnsgroin vaults, decorative arcading, and large towers. The walls carried the weight of the building instead of the arches. The design of the buttresses, vaults, and roofs were relatively more primitively looking than the styles which emerged later on.

Overall, the Romanesque design was described as being simple. Although it was considered as being very simple, it did reintroduce two major elements of fine art: stained glass and sculpture. Since the fall of the Roman Empire, sculptures have basically been abandoned, which is why their Romanesque revival was very much needed.

- Gothic architecture emerged as a development of the existing Romanesque style of architecture. It rose in popularity in the 12th century until the middle of the 15th century. It is mostly described as a form of architecture employing the use of pointed arches (its most defining feature), which is thought to have originated from the Assyrian or Islamic architectural styles.

The pointed arches in Gothic architecture were very significant because these introduced an innovation which was thought to be improbable with the Romanesque design. Gothic arches were much higher and steeper; therefore, they required the support of long and thinner pillars. This gave architects the freedom to make the vaults much higher, therefore creating the effect of the arches reaching towards the heavens.

- By the 15th century, the Age of Enlightenment has begun. Prosperity within city states as well as competition between them in the financial sense began, with important families beginning to be recognized, such as the Medici clan of Florence and the Fuggers clan of Germany.

The Renaissance was basically considered as the point in history when Europeans began to look back and appreciate the works of the ancient Romans and Greeks. The Renaissance architectural style drew heavily from these influences, while still maintaining some of the influences of the Gothic and Byzantine styles.

Not only did Renaissance architects such as Michelangelo Buonaroti and Raffaello Santi incorporated the Greek and Roman styles of building and designing the walls and roofs of churches, but they also incorporated mosaics and stained glass.

Some of the greatest examples of Renaissance architecture include the Basilica of Saint Peter in Rome, as well as the Chateau de Fontainebleu in France.

- The changes that followed the Renaissance era regarding the evolution of architectural styles simply revolved around the continuous process of resurgence of old styles. With changing political and philosophical atmospheres happening especially with the birth of Protestantism, grander and more dynamic versions of the Renaissance style emerged, eventually giving birth to the Baroque style of architecture.

The Baroque Style can be described as being extremely ornate, elaborate, detailed, and complex, compared to existing architectural styles. There were more swirl shapes incorporated into the designs, and there was much use of color, perspective, texture, and light manipulation. The main point of Baroque architecture was to elicit the feelings of grandeur and awe.

People, especially those who belonged in the lower classes, did not appreciate the extravagance of the Baroque design. Instead, they regarded it as a way to emphasize the richness of the rich and the poverty of the poor.

In France, the reign of King Louis XIV, which had been filled will so much grand ceremonies and rituals (Even his morning routines such as dressing up and eating breakfast were considered as important events by the nobility, and so many would spend money just to be able to get a glimpse, much more to serve, the monarch.) worsened the ire of the common folk, therefore forcing his successor Louis XV to tone down the style and begin an architectural movement which was simpler than the Baroque style.

Instead of focusing on outwardly looks, the Rococo style focused on interior design. The reason for this is because the movement itself mostly happened in France, and the nobility were not willing to spend money on rebuilding their massive chateaux. Instead of building new homes, they simply focused on making changes on what they already have in their current living spaces. This resulted in Rococo architects being considered more as interior designers than anything else. They concentrated on making rooms with decorations, filling them with murals, furniture, tapestries, mirrors, silks, and porcelain, which would give any person who enters the room a sense of grandeur. This in effect managed to prevent making the Third Estate angry because any changes to mansions that were made were not created on the exterior of the houses.

- The times that came after the rise of the Rococo style of architecture saw further revival of old styles, such as Greek, Gothic, and Neo-Romanesque architecture. These were incorporated into designs of not just buildings, but also of bridges and other public structures.

- It was not until the coming of Frank Lloyd Wright (1867-1959), the single greatest American architect to have ever lived, that the focus was not on style but on function. He revolutionized the design of domestic homes, focusing on the use of unfinished natural materials and the expansion of interior spaces. Plans made by Wright also introduced an open layout, which is still popular to this day. His works became the inspiration for the modernization of architecture, eventually leading to the birth of the architectural styles which we have today.

Chapter 3: Tools Of An Architect

Every profession has specific requirements. They require specific sets of skills, and they also require the people to have the tools needed in order to get their job done right. For architects, there are basic necessities which one must possess in order to properly execute their jobs every day. As a beginner, remember to have all of the items listed below.

1. Drafting Table – This is a table designed specifically for the needs of architects and engineers. A drafting table is a multipurpose table that can be used for any type of sketching, drawing, or even writing activity done on a large piece of paper. It can also be used to read large books or any other documents that have a large size. For architects, it is primarily used as the main workstation where both rough and final blueprint drafts are created.

2. Tracing Paper – As your work progresses, it will undergo a lot of changes. You will tend to eliminate or add elements in your drawing. Doing it all in just one paper can be messy, that is why a tracing paper is

something that you will need. Tracing paper is a type of paper that has low opacity, which means that it is transparent enough for light to pass through. Because of its low opacity, a tracing paper can be used to copy drawings precisely.

3. Lots of pencils and erasers – You will be creating lots of drafts and changes before you get to your final product, which is why you will need a lot of these. It would be great if you would purchase pencils with varying thicknesses and color, so that you will not find it difficult to distinguish lines from one another during the drafting process.

4. Compass – No, this is not the compass that is used for navigating. An architectural compass is a device which helps in creating perfect circular shapes. Drawing a perfect circle is extremely difficult to achieve, especially without a guide. Even if you manage to make one, that does not mean that you would be able to recreate the one you made. Compasses can be used to draw circles of all sizes. The pen can be adjusted in order to change the size of the circle you

are making. In addition, compasses also help create small holes in the paper.

5. Tape Dots – These are very helpful in keeping your blueprints firmly planted on the drafting table. Not only do they serve as a way to keep blueprints in place, but they are also helpful in keeping other types of paper from being taken by the wind, such as fine art and drawings. Tape dots normally come in very convenient boxes with a pull-tab design. They are very easy to use, and they will not harm the paper when you peel them off.

6. Triangles – Triangles are three-sided rulers which usually come with two sides of equal measurement that meet at a 90 degree angle. These two parallel lines are joined together by a third side, leaning at a 45 degree angle. Triangles are used to ensure that squares are drawn perfectly, and to determine where the bias lines are.

7. Scales – Architects do not draw everything in full size. Rather, they approximate, or use smaller measurements to represent bigger measurements (reading architectural scales will be discussed in another

chapter). You will also need scales or rulers in order to keep your lines straight and adjusted. As an architect you have to develop the habit of making your lines perfect so you'll avoid flaws.

8. Markers – Obviously, markers of all sizes and colors are needed by architects in order to indicate specific parts in their drawings. When you draw your first building blueprint, there is a tendency that you might become confused with the lines, especially if they all look the same. Lines come in different types (which will be discussed later) and thicknesses, which is why you will need markers with varying tints and thickness in order to make lines more distinguished.

9. Sketchbooks – Although primitive, this is a key tool especially for beginners. Before you purchase a fancy computer and install a complex program to help you with your work, you should first buy a sketchpad. This is where you will create and collect your rough drafts before you put the final products in a CAD (Computer-Aided Design) program. You will shape your ideas, take note of

architectural styles, and form your own designs in your sketchbook.

10. A Computer, preferably a laptop – This is not an actual necessity, but having this one is an advantage. Almost all architects find having a computer very useful. Once your work is completely laid out on a sketchbook, you will then need to put it in a CAD program, since making improvements in CAD makes editing and measuring your work a breeze. In addition, not only can it serve as your workplace, but it can also help you with research, such as when you are looking for inspiration in the different architectural styles.

11. Coffee – You are going to be spending hours upon hours creating and designing homes and spaces. Your work will take a lot of time to complete, and will also take a lot of your energy. You'd want to continue with your work without having to feel tired or sleepy, so a great way to stay awake is to always have a cup of coffee with you to boost your energy. Just remember that everything is bad when taken in excess, so do not drink too much

coffee. If you really cannot continue with your work, take some time to rest.

Chapter 4: Basic Concepts in Architecture

The ability to draw and form straight lines is only a part of the complete set of skills which you must possess in order to become a great architect. Aside from understanding the history of architecture's evolution, as well as having all the materials needed for the job, an architect should also keep in mind the most basic concepts of architecture.

Architectural concepts are the principles which serve as the core ideas which are considered in the creation and design of the world's greatest man-made structures and homes. Having an understanding of these basic concepts can be greatly beneficial to an architect who is only beginning to learn his craft, to an architect who is at the beginning of designing a home, and to an architect who is evaluating another architect's designs.

However, although these concepts are extremely fundamental, you should keep in mind that architecture itself is not solely based on these ideas. Remember that these only served as guidelines for architects, and they in no way should limit your imagination when you are designing.

This is a very huge topic, which is why we are going to discuss them in parts, beginning with the most basic going down to the most complex. Since we have already tackled the history of architecture, we will discuss the practical principles of architectural design. These principles are usually found in all designs. The principles of architectural design include the following: Color Theory, Texture, Balance, Scale, Gestalt Laws, and Gestalt Principles.

Color Theory

This is a theory which tries to explain how we as humans perceive and experience color. Basically, the common idea of people about color is incorrect. This assumption may be simple, but it actually has a lot of meaning behind it.

We have conditioned our minds to think that color is a physical phenomenon, that it is a real thing and that it refers to an object's condition. We were raised to think that color is something that can be interacted with, something that is innate in every single object in the universe, and that it is not susceptible to sudden and frequent changes. For instance, in the sentence "Bananas are yellow", the idea is that the yellowness of the banana is a natural characteristic of the fruit, as much as its weight is. However, the truth is that the banana's yellowness is heavily reliant on two elements: 1) the light which strikes the fruit; and 2) the person who is looking at the banana.

Keep in mind that weight is not affected by our perception of the object which possesses the weight. A banana will continue being light weighted even if we do not interact with it.

Regardless if the banana is located in a very bright or very dark room, its weight will remain constant. However, the same does not go with color.

You probably already have an idea from your elementary school days about the rainbow, and about the color spectrum visible to the human eye. The idea behind this concept is that our world constantly receives radiation from the sun and from the universe. However, in the vast scheme of this radiation, we can only see a fraction.

This radiation is perceived as being in the form of waves, and we can only see these waves in specific lengths and frequencies. For instance, a ray of light with a particular frequency may appear as red. On the other hand, another frequency may appear as green, and another as violet and so on. The colors that we see vary depending on their frequencies, which collectively can be seen on rainbows.

This concept, however, falls short in explaining why we see other colors aside from the ones which we actually see on the rainbow. For instance, in the rainbow, there is only one true red. However, we all know for a fact that red can come in different hues, ranging from dark to light red. Color theory tries to explain why this happens.

The colors which we see exist only in our minds. You may remember talking about the parts of the eye and how the eye works during one of your health classes when you were a kid, and you might remember learning that the eyes can perceive color with the help of very tiny cone-shaped sensors which sense a specific light frequency. One cone is sensitive to red frequency, another is sensitive to blue frequency, and the other one is sensitive to green frequency. However, these sensitivities are not exactly exclusive, and the cones can be sensitive to other frequencies as well, although not as much as to the one to which they are most sensitive.

We would be able to see much more than what the visible spectrum offers if we only had more cones in our eyes. Other animals have these cones which help them see light frequencies which our human eyes cannot perceive, such as ultraviolet and infrared. Practically speaking, we can only work with what we have. Therefore, color theory is only concerned with the colors that are seen and experienced by human beings.

Our eyes and brain work as partners in order to interpret the frequencies of light we receive into elements which we can understand. The eyes are responsible for actually sensing the light frequencies and the brain is responsible for interpreting the light frequencies and turning them into the color that we perceive. This process helps our brains build an entire spectrum of colors which far exceed what one rainbow can offer. Color theory is also concerned with the brain's interpretation of color and how it is able to understand and create different hues of just one color.

Color theory also tackles how our minds relate colors to people, events, and emotions. For instance, the color red is often associated by people with the feeling of rage, anger, lust, or love. It is also associated with objects such as apples, strawberries, and blood. However, it becomes very complicated for our minds once we begin to expose our eyes to one specific color, and then have that color suddenly removed from our sight, and then placed on a field of almost similar hues while being tasked to find that color again. Instead of vividly recalling the color that was seen, the mind slowly forgets the color and replaces the old memory with new memories of the new colors.

What color theory teaches an architect is to be very sensitive with color and to be always ready to make comparisons between almost identical colors. Color is an integral part in architectural design, and so it is important for an architect to be very cautious when selecting and grouping them, especially when the task is in regards to interior design, or when working with a theme or style.

Texture

When we talk about texture, we are referring to the skin of the structure. How a structure feels and what its walls look like are two things which describe texture. Humans have had entire lifetimes of experiencing texture both with touch and with sight. We have gained experience in associating how things feel with what they look like so much that even if we do not get to touch a particular object, we would be able to know how it must feel just by looking at it.

When it comes to houses, parts such as the roof would not be readily accessible to you. However, just looking at the roof would give you enough information to be able to conclude how it must feel when you do get to touch it. This lets us conclude that our sense of sight is as powerful as our sense of touch when determining the tactile feeling of particular objects, so much in fact that we only need our eyes to determine the texture of particular furnishings or designs.

In relation to architecture, texture can be achieved using the building's skin, or by placing pieces of a pattern together close enough in order for the entire pattern to look like one single texture, regardless if it is horizontal or vertical. The stripes which can be created can be as close as one floor apart, but when you look at the building from afar, it would look like the patterns create a unified pattern that takes on the image of a surface finish.

Buildings which are furnished with smooth concrete only have one type of surface. This surface type will continue being consistent regardless of what time of the day it is that you are viewing the building. When you cover that layer of concrete with ingrain made of pebbles, or stucco, you would be creating a texture that changes as the sun moves across the sky and as the shape of shadows changes. This type of texture is called surface relief, and it can provide a house with a look that change throughout the course of the day.

During the last few years of the Victorian era, homes utilized shingles which vary in size to serve as house decor. There are times when the shingles would be shaped to look like fish scales, but this was not done in order to express the house owner's interest in fishes, but is simply put in order to show a visually interesting texture to the house. Shingles entertain the eyes, and make the building where they are placed more interesting to look at.

Texture is a fundamental element in architecture. Texture is put on architectural structures mainly because of tradition, but also because a particular texture can evoke a specific feeling in a person who views it. For instance, building textures which look similar to lap siding are used because they make the building look home like and comforting. However, if you add corrugated metal to the lap siding texture, you would drastically change the feeling that the texture expresses into something which is very remote from being comfortable.

Balance

When we talk about balance within the context of architectural design, we are referring to a system of element distribution which looks pleasing to the eyes. Architectural design often associates balance with mass, but it can also refer to other elements which play equally important roles in achieving it.

As humans, we are designed to always maintain balance in our lives, regardless if it is internal or external. Internally speaking, we continuously seek balance by organizing how we spend time, and in setting our priorities straight. We also tend to move our bodies in ways which can not only make us feel more comfortable, but also in a way which can make us feel like we are balanced. In our minds, balance is simply feels right to us. Whenever we see something that is not balanced, the first reaction that we have is to find a way to make sure that that object's balance is returned.

When it comes to the visual arts such as painting, balance is always something that artists struggle to maintain in their works. Balance is always aimed for, and this can prove to be difficult because artists can only work in two dimensions. If the painting is intended to be realistic, imbalance may be perceived if the artist draws a fat man on the corner of the canvass when the only other element on the picture is a skinny man located in the center, making the position of the fat man awkward.

Architects maintain architectural balance by utilizing the concept of symmetry. Symmetry is a system used to maintain balance by putting elements of equal measurement on equal sides of a surface. Basically, symmetry implies that the elements on one side of a surface should simply be mirrored on the other side.

Symmetry can be achieved in many ways, and it can also manifest itself in parts of a building aside from the roof or the shape of the house itself. Symmetry can also be achieved by making sure that the windows are equally distanced. For example, you might be designing a home where there is no need for a window on the left side of a house, while there are rooms needing windows on the right. Although the left side does not need windows, putting windows there would make the house look better, especially if the number of windows on the left matches the number of windows on the right.

Scale

This principle refers to the relation between our size and the size of the world around us. Humans normally measure everything against themselves. Humans always use themselves as the standard for everything, even in taking measurements, especially if what is being measured is something which humans can use. This is exactly the reason why we have a unit of measurement called "feet". However, aside from this, there are also other scales to be considered.

Architectural design basically deals with four different types of scales.

A. Human scale is the scale which we are used to having. The human scale's measurement is only enough for a person, offering just the right amount of space. Almost all residential properties are created using this scale. The house's ceiling is neither too high nor too low.

B. Intimate scale is slightly smaller than human scale. However, it is not really that small. Sometimes the difference between the intimate scale and the human scale is so insignificant, sometimes just plain imaginary or subjective, that it is sometimes referred to as a sub category of the human scale.

C. Monumental scale is a type of scale which is much larger than the human scale. This is often reserved for buildings which serve important societal, religious, or political roles such as churches, malls, or palaces. They are very easy to spot because people would seem like ants compared to the size of these buildings. Buildings built in monumental scale often evoke feelings of awe from the people who view them.

D. Shock scale is a very rare form of architectural scale. It is rare because not only does it vary in size (can be smaller or bigger than humans), but also because since its purpose is to shock people, it is not created that often. However, works with shock scale have been seen both in works of art and architecture.

Gestalt

Gestalt laws and principles – The word "gestalt" is a German word which literally translates to "shape." However, in architecture, as in psychology, gestalt refers to someone's perception of something. Gestalt laws cover the basic principles which architects adhere to in order to determine how elements in a design will be seen by others.

Gestalt laws:

A. Emergence – This refers to our perception of things in wholes rather than in parts. For instance, when we see a house, we do not see the number of windows, the color of the walls, the number of doors, or even if there is anyone in there. All that we see is that there is a house standing in front of us.

B. Reification – This refers to how our mind manages to see more than what it is supposed to see. When we see parts, our mind tries to unify them and turn them to a whole. The entire process is so innate in humans that we often forget the features and just see the big picture, just like what is proposed by the concept of emergence.

C. Invariance – This Gestalt law talks about how humans can recognize things even if alterations are made on their size, color, and texture. Regardless if lighting changes or slight shape changes are made on the object, the human eye will still be able to determine what exactly it is looking at, or at least be able to generate an intelligent guess.

D. Multi-Stability – The concept of multi stability proposes that the mind automatically stabilizes the things that it sees without having to actually do something physically in order to initiate change. We are able to perceive and make intelligent guesses on what particular shapes or images represent.

Gestalt Principles:

A. Simplicity – Our eyes choose simpler interpretations more often than elaborate ones.

B. Similarity – This explains that we tend to compare things to other things and determine if they are similar in any way. This also explains the reason why and how we are able to group different objects together simply because or our ability to categorize them and sort them out by theme.

C. Proximity – This concept is related to our mind's ability to determine the distance of one specific object from our location.

D. Symmetry – This refers to the innate desire of our minds to make elements in a particular setting equal in all aspects, which is oftentimes achieved by mirroring an object in one location in the opposite location.

E. Closure – This refers to the innate desire of the human mind to fill in gaps, complete lines, and close openings.

F. Continuity – This is the ability to fill in details so that it would be possible to arrive at the simplest interpretation of the details.

G. Smallness – This refers to our mind's preference for smaller elements or objects.

H. Surroundedness – This principle refers to the belief that elements which are located around a central object are automatically considered as belonging to the background of the central object that they are surrounding.

Space

This architectural concept refers to the area where the project is to be made. It refers to the area which is occupied by items and structures. Depending on how they are being used in a project, space can either be positive or negative. A positive space is a type of space which refers to the area that is occupied by the work's main subjects, such as sculptures, shapes, buildings, and even landscape pieces. On the other hand, negative space is the area which does not receive interaction with the works' main subjects. It is also referred to as the unused or unshaped part of the project.

There is also a type of space called the implied space, which is a type of space that is left blank in order to suggest to the person who is viewing the space indirectly that there is supposed to be something placed on that space to make it complete.

Figure

Ground and Solid Void Theory – These are almost the exact same theory, with the difference lying on the weight of consideration to be given to the elements involved.

The Figure Ground theory suggests that spaces which result from figure placement must be treated equally with the figures themselves.

On the other hand, the Solid Void theory has almost the same proposition as the figure ground theory. However, this theory looks at the concept from three different dimensions. When solid items are placed on space, the contents of the spaces which are implied by the objects' placements are to be considered as equally important as the objects themselves.

Chapter 5: Drafting: Why is it Important?

Architecture is a constructive art. In this field, you are creating works which will benefit people for a long time. You might have obviously experienced walking the streets in the city, and thinking of how much as a kid you looked forward to going to the mall every time your family goes out to bond, and realizing that that mall is still functioning even as you grew up. In movies, you have no doubt seen a character which became sentimental upon entering a building which held so many memories for them.

You see, these buildings, these crafts of architects, have long stood the test of time, and have served as places where memories have been created by people of different ages and different backgrounds. As an architect, you are also going to be doing the same. Designing structures where memories will be made is your calling.

Now that you know the history of architecture, as well as the tools that you will need in your job, we can now begin to talk about the process of drafting, or of creating the first sketches of your work. This is the first and most important step in building design, because this is where you will put your ideas onto paper for the first time.

Architects always have a sketch pad with them. Remember that since you are a beginner, this is a fundamental tool you must have. Just like how painters always carry their sketchbooks and how authors carry a notebook with them, architects need this just in case inspiration suddenly comes upon them. However, with the coming of technology, computer software has also been used to aid architects in making their drafts. Before you create a masterpiece, you must first put your first few drafts in paper, and then improve on it until you get a product that you find suitable or will meet your taste.

Drafting is the most basic exercise that an architect does in his profession. Although computers are basically being used by architects today more than paper, leaving the latter looking like a dying art, you should still consider trying to draw on paper first. Our mental and physical interactions are more connected to one another when we make use of our hands when we are drawing, because of how natural the process is.

Drafting is an important facet in architecture because it is a training ground. "Practice makes perfect", as the old saying goes; even in architecture, this is very true. Imagine a world where you need to compete in order for your products to get attention so that you can be successful. Of course, when you are faced with tough competition, you need to give your best shots all the time.

When aiming to give your best, you really cannot afford taking risks. You must be extremely convincing in order to get the attention of the people you need to attract, beating others who may be as equally qualified, or even more qualified than you.

Buildings stand as an artistic expression of an architect. In addition, it is also the effort of contractors and their entire team in order to make the vision of the architect a reality. In making this come true, an architect does not need just words. Architects must present a complete plan, a perfect layout of what he wants, what is going to happen, what it will look like, and what benefit it will give to the people who are going to see and experience his creation. Therefore, this is why a lot of architects greatly rely on CAD drawings in order to express the details of their work without confusing anyone. Not only does drafting offer a basic blueprint of a plan, but it also offers a point of agreement amongst a team.

Before you go in making your plan on a software program, it would be best first if you straighten it out on a piece of paper.

Write down your ideas first in words. What inspires you? What image appears in your mind? What emotion or feeling do you want your creation to evoke or express? Put them in writing first in your pad.

When you have that written down, you can now start with making sample drawings. As you draw, make markings. Write on certain angles and edges why you put those elements there, what inspired you to make those designs, and what function they will serve. This process will probably take a while.

Take time in editing your work, and in making sure that you are completely satisfied with what you have accomplished. Architectural drawing is the most basic component of building design, playing an extremely vital role in the translation of an architect's design into solid reality. Traditionally, this process requires an accurate representation of the work to be made by the architect to be drawn in paper.

Once you have created your work, you can now transfer what you have drawn into computer software, which would generate a more accurate visual representation of your work.

Chapter 6: Line Types

Architectural drawing, both in paper and in the computer, follows a specific standard, especially with the manner by which lines are drawn. In order to distinguish different areas of a structure from one another, varying types and weights of lines are used. One of the most basic things that a beginner architect must master is the basic types and weights of lines.

There are basically two kinds of lines: object lines and symbol lines.

An **object line** is a type of line which is used to present the actual shapes of items or buildings. Object lines are only used for areas of a building and objects which will be physically built. There are two kinds of object lines:

> A. Solid lines – These are used in order to show an object's visible edges. Solid lines show all visible edges, and their thickness or weight can vary depending on the situation. Heavy lines are used for profile or cut lines, while light lines are used to emphasize elevation.

B. Dashed lines – These are created to represent an object's hidden edges, or to represent an upper floor from a lower floor's point of view. Dashed lines can be categorized into two basic types:

    i. Phantom lines are drawn to represent overhead constructions, such as roof overhand edges, ceiling height changes, exposed living area ceiling beams, or a balcony. Longer dashes are used when making phantom lines.

    ii. Hidden lines represent an object's hidden edges, or a completely hidden object. Examples of hidden objects which can be represented by hidden lines include a basement, the building's foundations, or basically an underground structure. These are drawn using short dashes in order to prevent any confusion when looking at the floor plan.

2. A **symbol line** is a type of line which is used to represent specific information such as direction, symmetry, and dimensions. There are five basic types of symbol lines. These include:

   a. Dimension or extension lines – These are solid lines which are drawn to represent a dimension's limits. Distances are written above each dimension line.

   b. Center lines – These are drawn to show objects that are symmetrical. These are usually drawn with alternating long and short dashes, or alternating dots and short dashes. Two center lines are drawn to show a round object's center.

   c. Dashed lines – These are drawn in order to represent alternate object positions, future structures, and swing door directions. Typically they are the half-curve dash line located in spaces in object lines, which are used to represent how a door would open.

d. Property or boundary lines – These are drawn with alternating pairs of long and short dashes. They are drawn to represent the limits of a property's land area.

e. Cutting plane lines – These are drawn to show how the entire section is being viewed. These lines are usually drawn as heavy lines that have pairs of short dashes and long dashes, forming a short–short–long pattern.

Chapter 7: Reading Architectural Scales

Architects use a specific type of ruler for their work; this is called an architectural scale. An architectural scale is a type of ruler which was designed in order to help architects determine a distance's exact dimensions on a scaled representation.

You obviously cannot draw the house that you are designing using the real measurements; just imagine creating a 210x210 foot home, and actually drawing a line that is 210 feet on a piece of paper. That is simply not possible. Almost all construction, engineering, and architectural drawings are scaled down so that large projects can be fit into a piece of paper more easily.

Being able to read and use an architectural scale is a fundamental skill that an architect must have. Before you begin using this tool, you must remember first that what is being measured in an architectural scale is the scale of a particular item or drawing. After you have determined the scale of the drawing you are going to measure, then you are going to choose the right scale on your ruler. For example, 1/8 on the ruler would represent one foot on the actual structure.

When choosing the right scale for your structure on your ruler, be very careful in your selection. This is because the architectural scale offers two separate scales, each located on one side of the ruler, with the manner by which you read them going in opposite directions.

The procedure in converting real measurements to scale drawings is somewhat complicated. Making things right in your drawings do not allow any room for guessing, which may negatively impact your work. To make sure that your measurements are indeed correct, follow the steps listed below and make sure that you practice as much as you can.

- Line up your scale's zero mark with the start of the item that you are going to measure.

- Identify at which point on your scale you wish to put the ending point of your item.

- Look at the number of the scale which is written closest to your determined ending point. Memorize this number, and always keep in mind that you should round down regardless of how close your ending is to the next number.

- When you are finished, you should have the perfect one-foot representation of the item which you are going to measure.

- Now that you know how to measure for full feet, you will now need to know how to measure fractions of feet. In order for you to add fractional feet for measurement, slide your ruler until the number you took note of lines up with the measured item's end.

- After doing this, return to the scale's zero end. The fractional feet that you are going to measure is going to be represented by the length between the measured object's start point to the scale's zero point.

- Read the number which you are going to get and add it up to the total number of feet that you have.

Chapter 8: Architectural Styles

The methods of expression that an architect can take can be vast. However, the designs that most architects follow are generally inspired by the works of architects of the past. Throughout the course of history, the design of buildings has been subject to so many different and drastic changes in style. Today, the architectural styles that we see in today's buildings have become a sort of way for us to see and remind ourselves of the fact that our tastes in styles and textures are in a constant change.

Architectural designs and styles have been mainly influenced by some of the greatest ancient civilizations in history, such as the Greeks, the Persians, the Romans, and the Egyptians. These civilizations have created homes, temples, palaces, and monuments which embodied their own cultures and traditions. Although the ways of the ancient people have long since been eradicated from modern society thanks to constant changes which took place in our history, some, if not all of the designs which they incorporated in their structure have survived to this day, and are now significantly influencing the minds of today's modern architects.

As a novice, you need to gain an understanding of the basic architectural styles so that you will find it easy to label your work's inspiration, and so that you would not be confused about which style should be best used for a particular place (because sometimes there are areas wherein one style is more dominantly used than others).

- Palladianism – This is an architectural style which belongs to the Classical genre. This was named after the famous architect from the Italian Renaissance, Andrea Palladio (1508-1580). Palladio's works held the most significant influence in the development of European architecture, beginning from the 17th century, up to the present day. Palladio's architectural style was basically grounded on being proportional and having perfect symmetry. He brought his ideas to England during the Jacobean Era, and from there the Palladian style further improved by incorporating styles from other architects of the Renaissance Era.

Palladian buildings can easily be spotted because of the attention to symmetry and proportion that is put in the designs. In addition, Palladian buildings also incorporate a specific design for windows, called Palladian windows (although they can also be called Venetian or Serliana windows). They also have a temple-like opening, and are mostly used as residential buildings or places of worship.

- Brutalism – This kind of architectural style is focused on raw materials. The main point of emphasis of brutalist architecture is on textures, materials, and construction. Because of its emphasis on these elements, brutalist buildings tend to have very expressive forms. The term "Brutalist" was first used by Reyner Banham, an architectural historian, in 1954.

Brutalist buildings have very significant characteristics, such as unusual shapes, massive forms, unfinished and rough surfaces, smaller than usual windows, and heavy materials.

- Art Deco – This architectural style was first seen in the Paris Exhibition Internationale des Arts Decoratifs in 1925. The style was inspired by the coming of the Machine Age, incorporating geometric elements as well as designs which are predominantly vertically oriented.

Although this style of decoration was barely used for residential structures, they were more used for commercial establishments during the 1930s. Hollywood movies dating back to the 1930s heavily popularized roofline projections such as towers, which further emphasized the vertical orientation of these buildings.

In addition to the towers, Art Deco structures are also popular for their metal window casements, flat roofs, and stucco walls that are adorned with rectangular cut outs. In the 1940s, the Art Deco design eventually changed into Art Moderne, featuring more curves and an overall boat-like shape. Art Moderne became popular in the United States thanks to the efforts of Eliel Saarinen, a Finnish architect.

- Bungalow – This architectural style which is commonly used for small and one-storey houses originally gained popularity in California during the 1880s, created as a form of reaction against the then more common Victorian architectural style. The word "bungalow" is a word whose origins can be traced back to India, where it originally meant "small home with thatched roofing. The Victorian style was seen as too elaborate compared to the simplicity of the bungalow style. After it had become popular in California, the style then saw popularity growing towards the Midwest, where it continued to be the most popular architectural style for housing even during the Great Depression.

The defining features of bungalow homes include small and covered front porches, and hipped, low-pitched gabled roofs.

- Georgian – This style has a royal ancestry, acquiring its name from four former monarchs of England who were named George. The Georgian style is modelled after the most elaborate and refined homes in England, and became the staple architectural design in British colonial homes in the 1700s.

Georgian houses are most certainly fit for a king, with their symmetrical looks, a decorative above the front door, and paired chimneys. The houses that survive to this day stand at two to three storeys tall, with the second storey of a Georgina house often having five windows lined up in a neat row.

- Cape Cod – This architectural style was used as the design of the very first houses to be established in the United States. The original Cape Cod homes stood one storey tall, were sided with shingles, and had no dormers. This style became even more popular in suburban areas during the middle of the 20th century. Today, Cape Cod homes are either square or rectangular in shape, can stand either one or two stories tall, may have shutters or dormers, and are usually made of brick or clapboard.

- Dutch Colonial – This architectural style was originally made by early German Pennsylvania settlers in the 1600s. Germans, who in their native language referred to themselves as "Deutsch" (hence the style's name), designed their homes with flaring eaves which can extend to as far as the porch area, thereby providing the house with a barn-like effect.

Originally, the homes had just one bedroom. If extra rooms need to be made, another one would simply be added to the end of the existing room, therefore providing the structure with a linear floor plan. A chimney is located on one of the house's ends, and the end walls of the house are made of stone. After declining in popularity during the 17th to the 19th centuries, it was revived in the 20th century when people became nostalgic towards their colonial history.

- Colonial – This architectural style was born during the American colonial era and had originally incorporated a lot of different existing styles. The Colonial architectural style draws inspiration from the Georgian, Cape Cod, and Dutch Colonial styles. The Colonial style is most often described as a structure with a rectangular shape, with bedrooms often located on the second floor. The windows of this house are often double hung, and have small square panes with equal measurement.

The late 1800s to the early 20th century saw architects borrowing ideas from the Colonial style in order to create Colonial revival homes which come with elaborate cornices and central hallways. The difference between Colonial Revival and original Colonial homes is that Revival homes are trimmed with green or black shutters, and are sided in white clapboard.

- Split-level – This architectural style is now more seen in the Midwest and in the East, where it has been a popular style since the late 1950s. The split level house is a type of Modern style which architects made in order to make more use of particular spaces in the house dedicated to socializing and sleeping.

The split-level house provides a more creative and multi-level choice for those who were looking for something other than the traditional two-storey home, which was popular in the 1950s. The lower floors of the house are devoted to social functions, which is why TV rooms and garages are often located here. On the other hand, the midlevel and upper levels of the house are separated in order to provide a more peaceful space for the people who will be living in the house, which is why bedrooms are situated in these floors.

- Contemporary – This architectural style is very easy to spot as it stands out from the other architectural styles with its long and tall windows, odd mix of wall materials such as wood, brick, and stone, and the obvious lack of ornaments. Architects came up with two versions of the contemporary style between the 1950s and the 1970s: the gabled type and the flat-roof type. The gabled houses had exposed beams. Both of these types usually stand with just one storey and are usually designed with the surrounding landscape in mind.

- Shed – A deviation from the existing Modern style, this is a favourite of architects during the 1960s and the 1970s. This type of house features multiple sloping roofs which go in various directions, therefore creating multigeometric shapes. The exterior cladding of this structure is mostly made of board, wood shingle, or brick. The front doorway is often downplayed, and the windows are always made small. The style, unlike the traditional and older architectural styles, offers no balance or symmetry.

- Prairie – This is a common architectural style in the Midwest, created by the greatest American architect of all time, Frank Lloyd Wright, in 1893. The Prairie style has two types: symmetrical, and asymmetrical. Symmetrical homes have box-like shapes while Asymmetrical homes are often low-slung.

Chapter 9: Feng Shui in Architecture

Even in today's modern society, old beliefs and practices still hold a significant amount of importance in our lives and continue to influence our thoughts and actions. Almost all people have a particular taste when it comes to designing their homes or places of work. However, their tastes can also be significantly influenced by what they believe in. Religion and ancient forms of sciences are some examples of the types of elements which significantly influence our decision making processes. One of these elements is Feng Shui which is a dominant factor taken into consideration in making decisions, especially in Asian communities.

Practices and principles involved in Feng Shui continue to have a huge impact on the work and design of architects. Although as an architect you might not have a deep grasp of the concept of Feng Shui, it is still undeniably valuable in your profession, and even great architects benefit greatly from the value that Feng Shui possesses. Even if you just dip your feet in Feng Shui, you would realize a lot of things which may seem contradictory to what you are accustomed to doing as an architect.

Feng Shui makes people believe in particular facts which then influence not just how they live their lives, but also how they create their living or working spaces. The design methodologies that are incorporated in Feng Shui are so different and so unique that creating a specific definition of Feng Shui itself from the point of view of an architect may seem impossible. However, upon borrowing from various sources which are more knowledgeable about Feng Shui, we can come to the conclusion that it is the practice or the art of organizing possessions and structures in a way which would harmonize with nature and with spiritual elements. The phrase "Feng Shui" literally means "wind-water", and is basically grounded on the Yin-Yang patterns, as well as in the flow of Chi, or spiritual energies, which can either have positive or negative effects. The main influences of Feng Shui can be seen in arrangement, placement, and orientation of objects.

Although some of the practices that are incorporated in accordance to one's belief in Feng Shui can baffle some, such as placing a statue of a three-legged frog on the house's entrance for instance, there are other principles that we can find admirable due to their attention to physical design and in their clear value. These types of principles are what architects find healthy and good to use. A great example of this is having the bed face south east, in order to face the sun as it rises from that direction, therefore creating harmony with nature.

We are not going to go deep in discussing topics concerning Feng Shui that should be left out for discussion in another book. The purpose of this chapter is not to ingrain in the mind of the novice architect the deepest and most complex topics related to Feng Shui, such as finding a house's energy map or Bagua, or determining the birth element of a person and determining the lucky numbers of people. We will, however, discuss ten of the most common Feng Shui principles that seem to stick around as general rules for many designs.

1. The most ideal proportion for a living space is a square, with rectangular coming in at second. Creating square spaces create functional relationships among the spaces inside the house. Not only that, the shape also encourages efficiency in energy plans, as well as in the use of basic building materials.

2. The front of the house should be clean at all times. When we say that the house's

front should be clean, it means that there should be no overpowering elements in your house door, and designs in that part of the house should be kept at a minimum. Yard tools, trash bins, and other forms of distractions must be located elsewhere, and the house number must be clearly visible by being written in a large and clear font (preferably Helvetica or Century Gothic). The principle of Feng Shui claims that the entrance of the house is where positive energies come in. Not only that, it is the first thing that you see in the house from outside, and so it must always convey the feeling of positivity and stress relief.

3. The entrance door quality determines the energy quality. Not only should house entrances be clean and welcoming, but the doors themselves should be made of the best materials and should have a specific characteristic in order to attract positive energy. Design-wise, entrance doors must be made of a solid material and should open in. It should also be brightly colored.

4. Work areas should be separate from rest areas. Although this is already a basic design principle even outside Feng Shui, this is still an important concept in Feng Shui that you should never miss. When designing and arranging the spaces inside a home, the home office must be clearly separated from the other areas of the house, especially the sleeping and living areas. Elements of design which may have a psychological effect on the person living in the house must be completely separated; no work-related designs should appear on living spaces, and no living or rest-related designs should be placed anywhere near work spaces.

5. Rooms should not be filled with clutter. Cluttered rooms prevent the natural flow of energy throughout the house. Not only that, cluttered houses become the home of cluttered and confused minds. Therefore, in order to keep the energy flow constant, obstructions should be removed. In designing interior spaces, an architect must always provide storage areas where items which may clutter the house can be placed. This creates a well-

organized, relaxed, and calm environment.

6. Eliminate unused items. Just like in number 5 above, this is a basic home maintenance matter. If you are not using something in your home, get rid of it. Unused items typically become the home of negative energies, and so should be eliminated. If complete elimination is not an option, at least provide a storage space.

7. The house must have natural light and ventilation. Architects who take Feng Shui into account in their designs should know that in order to keep the balance between man and nature, nature should be allowed in the house. Therefore, typical design techniques involve big windows with natural daylight and that are also operable in order to let in natural ventilation from outside.

8. The bedroom must face southeast. Or if the bedroom cannot be positioned in alignment to this measure, the bed should at least be positioned to align to this direction. A common Feng Shui belief is that in order to maintain harmony with

nature, the natural process of sleeping and waking up should jive with the sunrise and sunset. Although this direction may be altered depending on the home owner's Kua number, or what part of their lives they are trying to improve (happiness, love, wealth), a majority choose southeast because they wish to wake up along with the sun.

9. Sharp edges or corners, as well as protruding objects, should be kept away from pointing to the east. These objects include the dining room table, the sofa, and the beds. This becomes very easy to follow if you strictly adhere to the square (or rectangular) shape of the house.

10. The house's central area should be empty. This is done in order to encourage proper energy circulation within the house. Not only does this encourage positive energy flow, but it is also great design-wise since it allows the common spaces in the house to share the house's common square footage.

Conclusion

We have discussed everything that you need to know, and now you can begin designing your own home!

You are now equipped with the most basic principles and skills needed in order to begin your journey as an architect. Remember that as you think of and draw your designs, never forget to always utilize your imagination. It would be fantastic if you would adhere to some of the existing architectural styles and designs which have been explained in this book, but it would also be great if you'd use your imagination to create something new.

Remember that the point of being an architect is to create something that is both beautiful and functional. Everything that you design must be a mix of both.

Always keep your imagination alive. Find inspiration from your environment, from the works of past architects, and from yourself. Architecture is a science, but it is also a form of expression. Use your skills to create something that people will love and find very useful in their lives.

Thank you once again for downloading and reading this book.

Made in the USA
Middletown, DE
10 August 2017